WORDS OF LIFE

WHEN LIFE TALKS TO YOU, LISTEN AND LEARN...

DEEPAK PRINCE

Lord God Almighty be praised for helping me author my first book!

I dedicate this book to my role model & my beloved late grandfather Mr. A. Victor (Retd. Head Master; Guinness World Record Holder) & my late grandmother Mrs. Michael Ammal (Retd. Teacher) without whom I would not have been what I am now!

Contents

Contents

Copyrights

ஐ

"Words of Life" by Deepak Prince

ஐ

Author email ID: wdeepakprince@gmail.com
First Edition

ஐ

Preface

Most of our recent moments pass by in a hurry, running around the daily chores, scheduled meetings, unscheduled calls and enough issues from within and from around. We generally miss to hear what life speaks to us and what it wants us to listen.

When the noise of the routines is pushed aside, the voice of the life can be heard. Some of the lessons and learnings that I took from my life are shared here to have a quick glance of what all your life can talk with you.

The intention of this book is not to hurt anyone but to openly share my thoughts on a few life-giving words based on the good and the bad that life had blessed me with and helped me understand myself & others in a much better way. You can very well agree to disagree with me in a few of my thoughts. :) And some of these - you might know already, but there was none to remind it to you again for quite some time. The contents are kept precise to help you run thru this quickly, even daily as a reminder of how you can make your life awesome. Or keep this as a ready-reckoner on your table. I hope you love reading this!

ACKNOWLEDGEMENTS

I wish to start by thanking my wife, 'Priscilla Barathi' for her fullest support & motivation in bringing out this book in complete. Thank you so much, dear. My kids 'Immanuel Jacob Prince' & 'Manny Joanna Prince' are the sweetest part of my life who gave me the responsibility to look beyond the usuals. Love you kiddies.

I'm immensely thankful to my parents - 'Walter Prince' & 'Elizabeth Rani' - for their continuous support. I want to acknowledge the blessings of my late father-in-law 'Arulraj' and support from my mother-in-law 'Amalorpavamari'.

Special thanks to my paternal uncle 'Peter Prince' and aunt 'Jyothi Prince' for their guidance, support in my life & also for proof reading the book.

This section will be incomplete if I do not thank all my brothers, sisters & cousins and also my friend Naresh who encouraged me in the initial stages of authoring the book.

Finally, I want to thank all my family, friends, colleagues and relatives who were by my side during the ups & downs in various part of my life & helped me push my limits!

I

Self-Care

First & foremost, don't depend on others to care for you. Take charge of yourself! You need to fight for yourself - Or You might end up fighting with yourself

II

Take Control

Situations and things won't go out of your control when you are at the helm! Don't get controlled; instead, just control!

III

Prioritize

Prepare a prioritization list for any of your works. Be it professional or personal. And action out in that order of priority

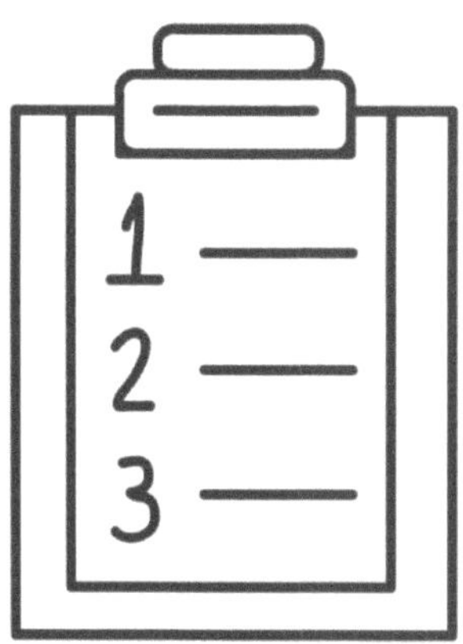

IV

Never Procrastinate

Later = Never; If you are deferring a task more than 3 times, then it is better to drop it and keep moving with the next

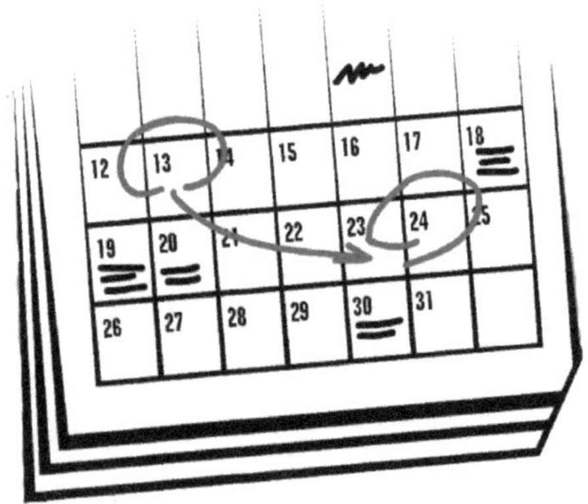

V

Trust Yourself

If you don't, then who would trust you?

You & You

VI

Timely Action

If you don't do your activities or take care of people on time (in any sense :)..), when things are under your control, then they will take control over you and you would be forced to do those activities and take better care of those people. If you don't decide, others will decide for you.

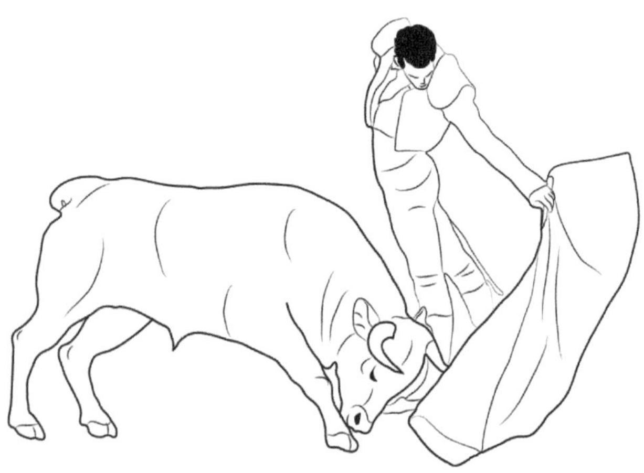

VII

Don't wait for time

Because time doesn't wait for you, you don't wait for it. Keep working on what needs to be done.

VIII

Take the credit way

Don't start your valuation of anyone with 100 points and keep reducing the score for their words and actions. Instead, start your valuation with 0 points and keep adding to their scores for their actions.

IX

Respect your enemies

Never under estimate the power of your enemy. It may be your Achilles' foot, one day. Respect their potential & stay cautious!!

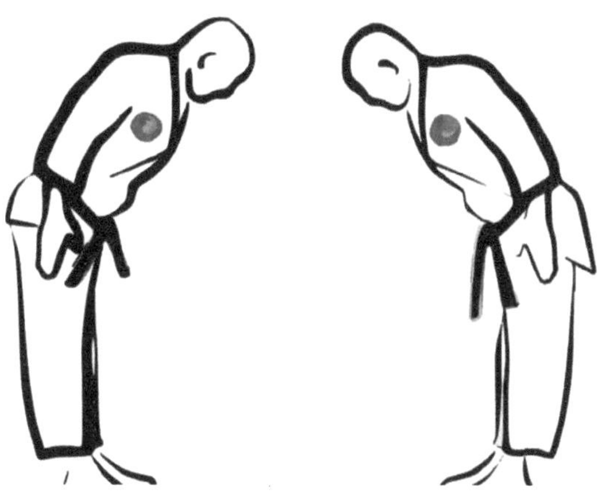

X

Disposition without delay

If you can solve a problem, solve it. If you can't, then move it to who can resolve it. Dispositioning is an art of achievers. Timely disposition will definitely keep you a winner! If you can do, do it! If you can't, then don't hold it!

XI

Focus on Life

Success and Failure are only mirages in desert. We need to ignore them and keep walking to reach the destination of a meaningful life. Focus on what you need to do; and never on what you don't need to do

XII

Be what you are!

You are not what others tell you are. But what you think you are, defines you and takes you further

XIII

Love your work

Start doing what you love and you will end up loving all that you do!

XIV

Schedule your day

Drive your day thru schedules instead of roaming without a plan

Daily Schedule

8:15 – 8:40am	G.U.M.s
8:40 – 9:45am	Reading
9:45 – 10:15am	Writing
10:15 – 10:35am	Recess
10:35 – 12:00pm	Math
12:00 – 12:20pm	ELD
12:20 – 1:00pm	Lunch
1:00 – 1:35pm	IWT
1:35 – 2:20pm	Content Areas
2:20 – 2:34pm	Class Closing

XV

Put your efforts

Sow your seeds of efforts in right place, at right time, in a right way and they will bring you their harvest on right season! Keep your head and heart in the right direction and don't worry about your feet. Good is not good when better is achievable and best is possible!

XVI

Persevere

Your attempts may fail, but you must never fail to attempt! It's not just about winning always, it's about persevering! A battery last longer only if it keeps flipping from full charge to low charge and then gets full charged again. That's how life leads us to make us stronger! Persevere in your downs

XVII

Self-Motivation

Motivation should be sourced from within and not from outside!

XVIII

Leverage Money's Potential

Money can't solve all the problems, but it can solve many problems! Learn to earn it, invest it & leverage it legally & ethically & morally. Make money to work for you instead of working for money. Don't be penny wise and pound foolish.

XIX

Don't shy away in asking questions

If you don't ask questions when you have the rights and authority, then you will be questioned to lose your rights and authority

XX

Cry when you need

One who cries is NOT the weakest one. And one who does not cry is NOT the strongest one. But never cry in front of those who made you cry!

XXI

Don't think yourself as a loser

No relationship cares for a loser. Only loser has to care for himself/herself. Only when he/she wins - all relations are happy and together and near. Always think that you are a winner & you will be!

XXII

First Preference

Only 2 persons can give u 1st preference. God and yourself. Live such that God can prefer you and do such that you prefer yourself

XXIII

Clean up your contacts

Keep cleaning up your surroundings of friends, neighbours, relatives, colleagues and people you meet around and disposing off the dusty ones. You will keep getting precious gems from hidden places who are really worth it!

XXIV

Follow your Spiritual time

If you are spiritual, follow a discipline to spend quality time between you and God. If you are not spiritual, take some time-out for being with nature

God made Earth and Me

XXV

Don't give up

Sometimes you would be pulled back to be taken to greater heights. Like how a compressed spring will jump above, when released. Trying situations calls for our inner most strength. So never panic when facing such moments. Instead focus on what needs to be done.

XXVI

Leave the lust

When lust calls for, run away without any second thought. And have a gateway on your eyes, for with eyes they enter on a greater extent.

XXVII

Practice

If you don't sweat in practice, you will bleed in war! This applies to anything you want to learn

XXVIII

Don't try to prove yourself

While doing right is difficult, proving that you are right is more difficult. So better don't waste your time and efforts in proving this to people who don't deserve it!

XXIX

Note your stress-busters

Quick stress busters - Hot shower, a long drive, a cup of coffee, movie time. What's your stress buster? Consciously note it & plan it - when you get packed up on your head.

XXX

Strengthen your will

Don't be like a glass of water which gets disturbed even for a breeze; be like an ocean which stays still even when a mountain is thrown into it!

XXXI

Choose a right mentor

Good mentors are like GPS while travelling thru life's journey. First pick the right mentor(s), then you are half done.

XXXII

You can't change others

This is a hard fact. Whatever you try. You can never be able to teach someone who is never ready to listen.

XXXIII

Learn to overcome yourself

Sometimes overcoming the world is very easy but overcoming self looks so much tough. You need to push yourself beyond your limits. You can keep improving to a better version of yourself each day.

XXXIV

Walk thru the reality

Never dodge to face the reality in any relationship - however it might be. It needs courage and strength to keep pacing. Some are blessed to stay together & some are blessed to move on! Once you are thru it, you will relieve yourself of unwarranted stress.

XXXV

Don't get carried away

Keep reviewing if you are unnecessarily working any sub-task instead of directly doing the actual main task itself

Don’t play fiddle when Rome is on fire - Like Nero did

XXXVI

Body is a balloon

Don't tamper your body or pressurize it more than it can bear. Once the balloon bursts, you can never blow it back again to its original capacity

Balloons with bandages cannot soar high

XXXVII

Don't lose your core value

Become strong but don't lose your core value. Transforming into a diamond from being a graphite is one of the tough phases of life, without changing what you are from inside. But don't get mixed up in the mean time. You need to have the same carbon element, to be a diamond as well!

XXXVIII

The Power of Compounding

Don't miss the power of compounding; Invest early!

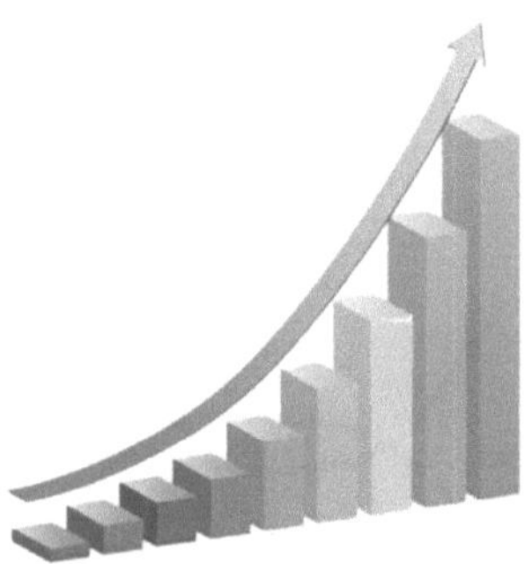

XXXIX

Face your fears

Fears are only virtual blockers from mind. Once you overcome, you will know how much a worthless thing they were! Batman was afraid of bats, but did he not overcome it?

XL

Commitment with hard work

Anyone can help you build your cocoon, but you should be receptive to come out as a butterfly with flying colours. You are not born to be a caterpillar or stay inside your cocoon. You have your wings to fly & explore the world. Just go thru the phases with courage & commitment & you will come out of it soon & fly high!

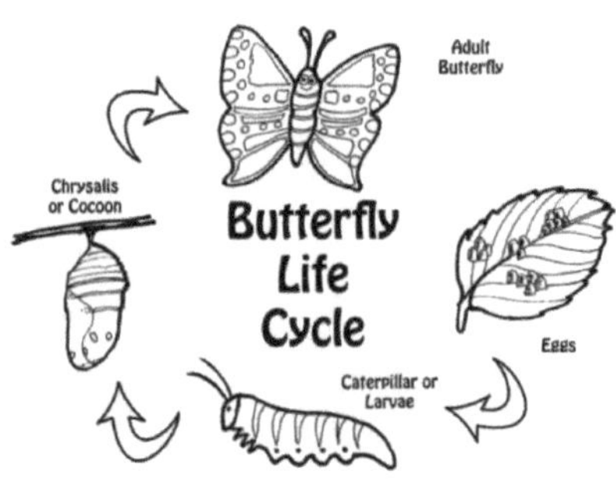

ABOUT THE AUTHOR

Deepak Prince is a Product Manager & Business Consultant by profession; Trainer by passion and an ardent lover of Nature who loves adding value to the people around. With the in-born empathy, he focuses on improving the quality of human lives thru his motivational discussions & thoughts. He is an Engineering and a Management Graduate with multiple accolades on work and loves to train & educate people on personal & professional fronts. This book is a part of such an inspiration!

ABOUT THE AUTHOR

Connect With Me Thru

deepakprince.com

linkedin/wdeepakprince

Notes

9 798887 045351

Printed by Libri Plureos GmbH in Hamburg, Germany